MW01137194

JEALOUSY

7 Steps to Freedom from Jealousy,
Insecurities, and Codependency

Table of Contents

INTRODUCTION

The story of jealousy dates way back into the early times of mankind. When people were not able to transcribe emotions, mythology kicked in and gave a boost with two passionate tales.

In ancient Greek mythology, the goddess Athena was known as the goddess of weaving. In light of this knowledge, Athena believed herself to be the supreme in that design league. And hence, when she heard that a farm girl called Arachne was a better weaver than her, she was jealous. Arachne was at the hands of a goddess, and Athena challenged her to a contest of spinning. In spite of her status, Athena lost, and in a spiteful rage ruined Arachne's work. Out of self –pity, Arachne hanged herself.

Athena was wrought with guilt and decided to turn Arachne into a spider.

Until today, when you walk along any dark corner, or through a grimly lit alley, you will find spiders still weaving.

Not one to have one talent, Athena was also the goddess of battle and wisdom. She was born in the most spectacular way; out of Zeus' head fully dressed for war. You see, quite often Zeus would sleep with many women, and his wife, Hera, the goddess of marriage and childbirth, would grow truly jealous and deal with the women with whom Zeus broke the rules of their marriage with.

As seen in the two tales, jealousy knows no bounds. Man or God, it breaks the chains of choice and affects any living being. Luckily or unluckily (you get to choose), jealousy doesn't follow one to the grave.

Or maybe, it does?

Your Free Gift

As a way of saying thanks for your purchase, I wanted to offer you a free bonus E-book called "*How to Talk to Anyone: 50 Best Tips and Tricks to Build Instant Rapport*".

Within this comprehensive guide, you will find information on:

- How to make a killer first impression

- Tips on becoming a great listener

- Using the FORM method for asking good questions

- Developing a great body language

- How to never run out of things to say

- Bonus chapters on Persuasion, Emotional Intelligence, and How to Analyze People

To grab your free bonus book just <u>tap here</u>, or go to:

<u>http://ryanjames.successpublishing.club/freebonus/</u>

CHAPTER 1

WHAT IS JEALOUSY?

It is that eight letter word we all have an inclination to walking away from. Some love it. Some hate it. Some embrace the power of it. In a word, it can make or break a foundation that has withstood and weathered the storms for years, and just because of a few actions are done out of spite and without thinking.

Jealousy isn't a pleasant word to use either. In many communities, it is frowned upon, though it can be used to spark a relationship in tatters (we shall look further into this later on). It is among the bottom half of all the words used to describe an emotion, the kind of emotion that leaves one in tears and feeling emotionally tired. Therefore, it can be said that jealousy is an emotion that erupts to be used negatively or positively when in want of something or someone owned or loved by someone else. In this case, we shall refer to jealousy between people and things.

It is not to be confused with envy either, dear reader. I'm sure that was where you were headed but cool your boots. Envy is described rather efficiently as "the resentful or unhappy feeling of wanting somebody else's success, good fortune, qualities, or possessions". You see, envy is closely similar to jealousy but different in the sense of what that feeling is gauged towards.

Even though jealousy can be quite a painful emotional experience, well resourceful psychologists deem it as an emotion that begs to be noticed- as a wake-up call to action, to save a treasured relationship in danger of becoming obsolete, and measures need to be taken to take back the affection of a loved one. In this regard, jealousy is an important emotion, as it conserves social bonds, and motivates people to engage in etiquette that maintains a significant connection. It only depends on how well it is handled and manipulated into doing good and not turning it into a physically forceful tool.

An example always places things into wider perspective. Let's say a bloke named John finds out his girlfriend Jenny has a nerdy best friend called Tom, and she is cozying up to him in ways that he finds uncomfortable, and in ways that she doesn't to him. Now we cannot say that John is envious of Tom, but he is way jealous of him. However, in the case John had the amazing computer and sleek DJ skills; it would be wise to say that Tom is envious of John.

There are several misconceptions surrounding jealousy, and this book would prefer setting those myths in order. It is high time for the facts to be laid down properly with no stones left unturned, to uncover the who, what, when, where, why, and how of jealousy. It is believed by many to be a purely negative emotion, but for the most part, it is not. It is wholly natural, and should not be seen as a beast that arose from eating too much gluten or trying out a different hair conditioner. It is purely a part of our DNA, and it proves a healthy relationship. Without it, without that fear of losing a loved one means we do not care. This breed of jealousy isn't what hurts relationships, but its companion, nay, and sibling, obsessive jealousy, does.

The second myth is that jealousy takes off the steam in a relationship. What this implies heavily is that jealousy finds a way to bring back the zest in a relationship, particularly a romantic one. It's a little bit tricky to generalize the individual reactions to a jealous significant other, and therefore, a little spice of an ingredient called jealousy can strip away the complacency heavily found in most long term relationships and serves a cold reminder never to take a partner for granted. As I said earlier, a little jealousy is a spice, more like chili. It can serve as a major turn on.

When we are in a relationship, we have the strong belief that our significant other should not talk or hang out with other guys/girls, now in this one, most of us are guilty as charged. This kind of belief is a heresy! In a healthy relationship, there should be support and encouragement to make friends of any gender outside the relationship and keep them. However, boundaries should be set in such a manner as to convey respect, but both partners should have fulfilling friendships with other people.

This one goes into the nasty obsessive kind. Going through your partner's phone and social media is

NOT okay. It is the exact opposite of all that are good and normal in a relationship. In any normal and working relationship, whether long distance or one in which you are so close to each other that you can hear them breathing at night, talk about your feelings. There is a sense in approaching your significant other in an open conversation rather than a confrontation.

Only the morals can be challenged with this one- not trusting your significant other, who has had priors in cheating when they say they are being faithful. It is quite natural for you to be hurt by dishonesty, but it is unjustified to use their past against them. Trust is something we choose to give, and it is quite unfair to both parties if one of you clearly doesn't trust the other. If it comes to the point of asking yourself if you trust your partner, always consider what it would take for them to earn your trust back. If the answer falls back on calling or texting them to see what they're up to, trust levels are really low there. If it so happens that your answer is to re-check yourself and adjust your attitude and etiquette, then a healthy relationship might bloom after all.

When an occurrence such as your partner being jealous of other people talking to you, and you find yourself thinking that it is protection they're offering, think again. Healthy relationships include healthy friendships. If your significant other tells you not to talk to other people, then that is a sign of bad faith-they do not trust you. It is an assertion of power and control, which can turn ugly and even abusive.

Seventh myth busted (boy, we are on a roll today!) - Jealous people carry the insecurity bug. Not the ladybug, but the dark cloud hovering over them - making them feel that they are being cheated on even if they are not. Being jealous is primal instinct, and in its own way, it's all about being in touch with our own emotionality. Forget about the crossed elbows and not-talking-to-each-other-scenario. A jealous partner who is aware of it may be meekly appreciative of the importance of their significant other to them. Clearly, we live in a world of a sea of change, a world where stability with family or workplace relationships or durability are all smoke and mirrors. A partner is an irreplaceable star.

Onwards and upwards I always say. Another myth is that jealousy leads to unruly behavior. It doesn't have to be implied like this, but it becomes a problem when someone doesn't know how to handle the emotions brought along by jealousy. We as human beings have the brains and power to make choices and control emotions.

Finally, the last misconception is that it is wrong to share feelings of the green-eyed monster with your partner. Nay I say, nay! Deep and meaningful love flourishes on transparency, honesty, and vulnerability. By opening up and saying what you truly feel emotionally, you are in actual fact saying that you care about your partner and would not know how to live with yourself if you lost such a precious part of your life.

It is quite troubling to find that an occurring ideology with people in general that it is a sign of strength and character to hide our insecurities and fears- put on a mask if you will. This common knowledge can perpetuate unfathomable heavy damage. It destroys true self-esteem and lays our relationships to waste.

Wisdom is realizing that acting strong is still acting. At times, we all really pretend to be something we're not, we leave our true selves in the dark and put on a mask. This, as common belief puts it, is done in an effort to control what we aspire others to think of us.

Ergo, we camouflage and hide our true selves to seek the admiration of others when trying to avoid their displeasure and when we betray do this, we are only betraying ourselves.

Human beings obtain self-esteem from the relationship with our own selves. Manipulating our personality to gain recognition from others leads to a term called other-esteem as it does not come from the inside. The more we look for approval from others, the more dishonest we become with ourselves. The end result will drastically affect us and lead us away from authentic self-esteem. Clearly, this is the polar opposite of the actions we should be taking- embracing and holding on to our vulnerability. What vulnerable in this sense of the word means is frankness. This does not allow you to twist it to mean fragile or weak. Human beings experience emotions that make us feel like an open wound ready to be attacked again, emotions such as insecurity, doubt, and fear. In truth, these are valid emotions, however, due to our twisted and deluded ethnic expectations that demand the face of strength, we decide to mask these feelings from each other. This, in turn, leads to us living our lives falsely thinking that our inadequacies are unique to us, and forget that others go through the same sense of fear that we feel.

Wearing a mask to hide your true self to the world is what entails you being breakable. Accepting who you are as a person makes your strength reverberate from you and echo out into the void. It never matters what other people think of you. Never. Only your thoughts and actions matter, for now, and ever more. This is the highway to a normal and powerful anchor in your self-esteem.

Nobody wants to be judged. That is understood. However, becoming an introvert and finding your way into unhealthy hobbies such as writing creep comics in the dark web to satisfy the need to be appreciated (and finding out that the only readership you have is anonymous individuals living in their mother's basement) is neither helpful nor beneficial.

The moment one accepts themselves as they are with their flaws and ugly scars, that is the time to realize that there is no point in hiding your true self to the world, and this is what constitutes a strong core in morality. Embracing the fears and judgment you expect from the outside world and turning them into your strengths, that's what living is all about.

The only one who can judge you is your inner self. No one else has that right, well, unless you find yourself in a criminally inclusive situation. That, my friend, is a charge you will have to face, a jury of your peers.

A common term is self-abuse, which means the ability to inflict emotional pain on oneself by using the pain from the actions of others upon you. Avoiding the hurt of inflicting judgment upon yourself is the whole point of you reading these words, and to learn how to maintain a level of pride in your personal achievements, however little or inconvenient to you.

Remember always, that you are one in a seven billion (and soon to be eight million!), so quit judging yourself, quit listening to other's advice about who you are as a person and quit comparing yourself to other people.

Think of carrying an egg in your purse for months believing it to be a perfect incubator for it, but you end up with a naughty smell wafting through during an important meeting at work. Similar to that reference being made in light of a sense of comprehension that might not be there.

It is pointless.

It is a game of madness that we keep playing with ourselves, a game in which we shelve away the very qualities that make us special and unique in our loved ones' eyes and that make us more powerful than we could ever fathom.

The game needs to change.

CHAPTER 2

TYPES OF JEALOUSY

There are two cases of jealousy, most common to the human race; reactive jealousy and suspicious jealousy. The difference is uncannily necessary, as almost everyone feels reactive jealousy when one assumes that their significant other is cheating, though people vary their inclinations to feel suspicious jealousy in the lack of any real risk. In both forms, a lot of hurt can take place in the relationship and once words are flung, they can never be taken back.

In describing the two cases one at a time, reactive jealousy, as it clearly ascribes to its name, is the type in which action takes place and not the kind in a cool sci-fi film. It's a survival and primal instinct humans have encoded in their DNA; to react to perceived danger to their loved ones.

When describing suspicious jealousy, it is in regard to a lack of evidence in foul play in the relationship. It occurs when one party in the relationship feels that there is a threat about to come into the relationship, but there is nothing to show for it but cold shoulders and rolled eyes. A case study example could be a simple wink or a smile or a flick of the hair from the lady in the television to your partner while watching Family Feud, and you feel a little bit uneasy from that. This might be a little overboard and dip into paranoia which shall be tabled in this chapter, but it is one that is based on senseless falsehood.

These two cases of jealousy are further split, and are a little bit of each other emotionally but wholly different with the scenarios in tow. Let's go into the details, shall we?

Normal Jealousy

a) Workplace jealousy - Jealousy in the workplace arises between colleagues competing for the same type of position, especially when a promotion comes up.

Though at times it can be deemed healthy competition, some ethics to be considered in the workplace are usually not put into play. Workplace jealousy can get quite rough as competitors go for the jugular in order to get that salary raise. If one colleague feels that another received, but was unworthy of, a salary increase or a title promotion, they may experience jealousy. They may feel especially jealous if they felt that they worked more diligently to earn accolades that were only given to the other person, and also when the appreciation of effort made is lacking. Often, this creates a feeling of disappointment and jealousy in the heart of an employee.

b) Sibling rivalry - Members of a family normally compare themselves to one another. The universal form of family jealousy is sibling rivalry, which affects brothers and sisters of all ages. There is a general sense of competition amongst children to be their parents' favorite child. It is a case of instinct and devotion to the parents in question. Siblings may compare their successes with one another, contest for the most of their parents' affection, and struggle to play with the same toy. There is also a display of jealousy on the arrival of a newborn and being made to share most of their toys with them. In layman's terms, it's a situation that can be a real pain in the neck. Sibling rivalry can be felt in an instance where one sibling is more successful than the other in school or career, but it may also be undergone if one sibling has a disability that requires extra attention from other family members. The comparison between siblings also brings a divide between the children.

c) Romantic jealousy- This is the one in which we all can agree to have experienced at one point in our lives. It leaves one with raw pain and a nasty taste in one's mouth. When two people come together and make the choice to be in a relationship together, even the slightest inkling of a perceived threat to the relationship can cause serious implications such as breaking up, or in cases where partners are mental, physical distress. This is where the term schizophrenia and delusion come to call.

d) Platonic jealousy - This is the special kind of jealousy that arises in friendships due to the same insecurities found in other relationships; the feelings of judgment, a fear of being substituted, and feelings of competition. Two female friends may discover that they are attracted to the same man and claim that neither will "go" for him. Nonetheless, they may both begin to feel all three jealous insecurities concurrently; they may feel competitive to earn the man's attention, insecure about their individual abilities to win him over, and fearful that the man will ultimately act as a friend replacement. In most cases, this kind of distrust may be confused with romantic kind of jealousy, but it should be remembered that there is a fine line between the two emotions. Tight bonds with friends can be so glued together that one party cannot see their lives moving forward without the other.

d) Abnormal jealousy - It is an unjustified kind of a jealousy caused by no possible reasons except for psychological issues such as hallucinations, obsession, or schizophrenia. Under some extreme cases of abnormal jealousy, a person is known to display immaturity and insecurity as well as a controlling vibe. Such people tend to assume that their family members, friends, and partners are unfaithful to them. This kind of jealousy is usually described with words like gruesome, compulsive, or apprehensive. It can be accredited to extreme immaturity, insecurity or an obsession with being in control. Sometimes it is due to a mental illness such as schizophrenia or paranoia or caused by a chemical imbalance in the brain. This is mostly referred to as delusional jealousy in learned and medical circles.

In 1991, a bright fellow named Gerrod Parrott claimed that the clear distinction between all these levels of jealousy is the kind of threat imminent to that said relationship. In other words, what he meant was that for you to know which level of jealousy you are in, it would be a wise choice to clearly understand the level of perceived or real threat that will attack your relationship. If the occurrence of a threat is justified and there is solid proof of foul play in the relationship, then it can be truly said to be rational and precautions should be taken for it not to be reactive. However, if the claims of jealousy are only by imagination and cannot hold water in any way, then the only threat is imagined and can only result in suspicious jealousy.

Finally, the long hurdle of the types of jealousy comes to a halt. Several if counted one by one, but it's necessary to understand the different situations that may arise significantly in daily life. Be it a barbecue session with the family, workplace event, church group, or even prize giving day at school. Coming to terms with the level of jealousy you are in is a brave step in coming clean and healing the relationship severed.

Now you are in the know of the categories as they are with different types of relationships, with some familial and others professional. All in all, the effects and consequences are real, and we shall look further into this in the coming chapters.

CHAPTER 3

SELF-ESTEEM AND JEALOUSY

The two flow in the same river streaming in the same direction, and can collide if not steered properly away from each other. A new study conducted and published in Addictive Behaviors found out that people who depend on their relationship for self-esteem most commonly turn to alcohol once the green-eyed monster hits them and hits them hard. The research is the initial study to show the correlation between romantic jealousy, relationship-dependent self-esteem, and alcoholism. That was a mouthful, but in clear layman's terms, this means the link between steamy jealousy, clingy relationships with the result of low self-esteem, and nectar of the gods. The researchers from the University of Houston say that understanding the link between these three factors could help identify people at risk of alcoholism.

Different people deal with their stress in different ways, some run, some hit walls, others write it out, and few scream into the pillows and sleep it off. None of us is the same as the other. For some people, alcohol is go-to for pain relief. Don't get me wrong, a glass of the good stuff is fun and splendid with a friend after a hectic day at the office and shared with limits, but using it to deal with emotions is hard enough as it is.

Jealousy between two lovers is an event most couples would not appreciate experiencing, and an underlying issue is how little work has been put into researching how abuse of alcohol is related to it. Luckily, a study was done to demystify the correlations between these three. Studies prior to this one only researched on the link between alcohol abuse and jealousy, and therefore this was the first one to link the three- self-esteem, jealousy, and alcohol rage-together.

So, the buddies of high science and philosophy at one University gathered a group of 277 volunteers, of whom 241 were women (clearly women are more responsive to their emotions than men, hence the bulge in number), and asked them questions about their self-esteem issues with regard to how high it relies on their relationships on and off campus.

As expected, the ones with clingy issues to their relationships and their partners often turned to alcohol to deal with these emotions. For the participants who were in a state of buzz kill and non-activity to advance in what they were currently doing in their relationships with their partners, this was true.

Alcohol seemed to be used in high levels when suspicion arose in relationships. If a partner felt or imagined their partner cheating, they turned to alcohol for some numbing or courage to confront them about it.

Another study was conducted at Pennsylvania State University by a certain curious psychology professor named Jeffrey Parker. Parker researched the benefits of intimacy between children and their close friends, in order to understand levels of intimacy that are coupled with vulnerability, which may prove a relation between pessimism and jealousy.

The team at Penn University led by Parker assessed almost 500 5th to 9th graders who had some documented issues with themselves and others, issues pertaining to jealousy. This was done to achieve comprehension of teenagers' weaknesses and susceptibilities to jealousy.

A series of questions was designed for 27 willing volunteers (for no pay at all, which was very mature of them if I do say so myself). What was found in the questions was very peculiar and increasingly interesting as they went by, questions assessing how the volunteers felt when their best friends chose someone else to go shopping with or do an activity without involving them.

Beyond the scope of this study that was divided into two parts, the researchers questioned the volunteers' popularities for being ones to hold a grudge on a classmate by asking their peers at school to evaluate them.

This is what the study found out;

Those girls (not too obvious, huh?) held the reputation of high jealousy levels than boys. This is because girls tend to expect affection (kindness, care, and an occasional carrying of their books all day) in their friendships more than boys did.

It was also found out that girls became more aggressive when it came to dealing with hormones. In this case, they shoved more and hurled really mean words to others if things didn't go their way. However, both boys and girls were both passively and actively aggressive when jealous.

Both girls and boys pointed out their jealousy tendencies to being lonely and not having someone to talk to and air out what they are going through.

Most teenagers have an irrational fear of disloyalty and unfaithfulness in their relationships when they decide to have them, with this, fear of being replaced by their friends is high. Hormones and high levels of caffeine and activity during the day tend to lead to this.

It was noted down that most teenagers have an inability to hold their friendships and relationships for a long period of time due to the fear of being replaced, leaving them feeling lonely and unapproachable on the inside.

Way past the times of modernism and free thinking, people thought that jealousy was a high case of being strong and having a high self-esteem. Yet the fairer sex has been proving it time and again that jealousy is a true sign of low self-esteem, especially in the dawn of the 21st century.

Does this theory make any semblance close to the truth?

Yes.

It really does.

Jealousy is a real sign of truly having a low self-esteem, and in the following chapters, there are certain remedies for that bad case of the green. Finding yourself in those chapters is bravery only for the few.

It is with high hope that the research done will help you, dear reader, to manage and knowing how to enslave the end results might be for you if it ever comes to the point of high alcohol consumption because of an emotion unfounded and constructed with fear and instability in a relationship.

It is important to note that jealousy and low self-esteem are in no way the same. One can inflame the other and fuel it to ridiculously high levels. The difference in both emotions is how you deal with them, positively or negatively, for which the ultimate choice solely lies in your hands.

CHAPTER 4

WHY ARE YOU JEALOUS?

A tinge of jealousy in a relationship is natural and at times described as healthy. Funny isn't it, that a thing that could break down the strongest of relationships to its knees is regarded as healthy. In several countries all over the world, jealousy is a matter that the older generation laughs about with each other as it is an emotion they learned to deal with over the years, and only the youth find it a milestone to take it by the horns. All over the world, jealously brings relationships to their knees in regards to being heated over if they are not. That tiny tweak of jealousy in a relationship is a feeling most people can relate to. We all feel that bout of jealousy due to the sense of losing that special connection we have with someone and he/she might find someone to replace us. Most people feel it on very few occasional basis, while there are those special collections of people who feel it to an unreasonable standard.

Well-established psychologists and scientists in kind over the decades have taken their time to study the origins and effects of jealousy. In some cases of research, it was found out in 2004 that jealousy may have a physical connection to the body differently in the genders.

To be more accurate, in 1995 it was decided that there is a specific layer of circuitry in the brain that encompasses jealous reactions, and discovered men were overcome by jealousy about a physical adultery, while women were hurt more by emotional perfidy (in as much as most men deny this fact, it is very true on all levels).

What follows in the next few statements is why you might find yourself jealous, and if you find that you relate to most of the situations, know that you are not alone.

Insecurity

Undoubtedly, this is the one that gives most relationships the shivers when thought of. The term inferiority complex is commonly used to reflect the primarily damaged self-esteem of a partner who is conflicted with jealousy.

It is intriguing to note that people in power, leaders, politicians, and those who hold office in authoritarian roles are not exclusive of this mentality. It gets to anyone anywhere, and since it feeds on love and hate at the same time, it finds itself quite the meal in almost every household.

Compulsive thinking

It is common for those who are diagnosed with OCD (obsessive-compulsive disorder) not to understand why their partners would cheat on them, let alone comprehend the feelings of jealousy. However, their brains tend to function compulsively into overdrive, and this is the case for clingy types of people. Anyone diagnosed with the disorder can confess to you how difficult it is to manage the fear of the unknown. They can come up with the oddest of stories about their partner's infidelity, completely unfounded and based on suspicion.

A case of distrustful personality

Paranoia is as severe as you would believe. Don't let it fool you; it can arise from the smallest of issues, even those which are as meaningless as going to browse on the toilet with your phone. Since it takes the form of schizophrenia in many circumstances, the high number of individuals diagnosed with this mental case lie on the less noisy side of this battlefield.

Several people in relationships today have some paranoia in short bursts, but not in the severity of the real disorder in its own right. Mild paranoia in couples or relationships proves great difficulty in having trust with one another. Quite often, they perceive lies and firmly believe in treachery in the relationships they have.

Reality smacks you in the face with a glove.

Ask a child with crumbs all over their faces if they ate the cookies and they will give you so many reasons as to how the cockroaches and rats came into the house and took them away and ran off on holiday before they got them.

Long story short, a jealous person will defend themselves when asked why they were jealous. It could be a series of incidences or just one remote incident. It is fair to place labels on a person who has had serial cases of jealousy as a jealous person by default if they cannot justify their claims of cheating.

When it so happens that there is no prior case to jealousy with you in your previous relationships, then the case of current jealousy in your relationship is not problematic. You're just being worried and apprehensive, and this is natural and should not make you feel belittled.

In conclusion, jealousy holds one hostage most times when felt, even when you know it does not make sense. Most people could go so far as to say jealousy is a companion in troubled storms, a friend to hold at the end of the world. To be fair and true, jealousy is an emotion to be felt whether we want to or not.

It is a great show of maturity to overcome innate feelings of jealousy. Understanding how the connection between you and your partner resonates is a way to swerve through the murky waters of suspicion and infidelity and rise above into the light of commitment and trust.

A relationship without jealousy holds no spark, no passion, and no divine bond that keeps the connection eternal. If there is no jealousy then it means you are a vampire- being able to switch off emotions like a light bulb whenever you want, and that hunger to be together no longer exists.

All over the world several communities have labeled jealousy as a natural reaction between loved ones when something revered is tampered with, say communication within the household. This is where universal truth got it all wrong. Jealousy is part of being human, and you have to embrace it.

Social norms dictate some very queer rules. Men feel biologically favored to have several female counterparts, and society backs them up. They are actually patted on the back for cases of infidelity in most cultures, but for women to be in the same position, society curses them out as outcasts and women of low self-respect.

Why?

The world is a weird place, that's why.

With all the rules dictating that for two people to get married the 'arrangement' has to be conceded by a judge and have witnesses to assess the proof of that 'arrangement' is utterly preposterous. When it also comes to the unfortunate case of marriage not working out, divorce has to be overseen by a judge and in both instances; the government has to know the things going on with this issue. A real Big Brother no one ever asked for, right? And in all these, you cannot do it yourself, at all.

Tagging of labels onto something as divine as a relationship brings to light the unnecessary nature of it all. 'Sweet' tags such as, "Till death do us part", "She is mine", "Don't you dare touch my man", "I own that girl", are so wrong, and are some of the reasons and causes of jealousy.

If all this is considered into current relationships, you may find why jealousy creeps into them by default. The truth of the matter is the only person whose actions you are truly in control of is yourself and no one else. All those self-help books telling you how to 'keep your man' or 'never letting her go' or 'how to make sure she can't wait to see you after work' will not work. Separation can and will happen at any time, and not remedying the cracks in the wall will end the relationship without a moment's notice.

Looking deep into the matter of roots of jealousy, the following are some of the reasons, mostly theories, as to the origins of the emotion in various relationships:

1. Biologically speaking

a.) Regarding sexual and romantic jealousy

Reproduction is a strong motivator for people to keep on surviving in this world. Not only is it fun practicing having children, but also the drive to be overprotective over 'their' women (see what I meant with the labels?). The need to reproduce and sire the next generation means the birth of jealousy when the chance of a mate being stolen by another arises.

Thinking from a female point of view, which in this case puts things in greater perspective, being cheated on means that her mate slacks in providing the basic needs for her, and his infidelity, in turn, means fewer assets for her and her offspring.

That went a little Neanderthal, but is relevant even today.

b.) In terms of the things of this earth

A material possession being prized over by human beings is uncommon to none. We like shiny bits, and we know that at specific moments in life these things mean our survival. It is therefore not common to find jealousy surrounding the lack of availability and loss of certain material wealth. This is linked to superior genes, and in this case, the term survival of the fittest must definitely be used.

We always want to win in everything. It is just primal and there is nothing to really do about it. It can even be seen in children as they get a new toy or game of cards. They throw a tantrum when they lose and run around naked when they win.

All this is linked to us wanting to survive better and longer.

2. Onward to the mind waves and their expanded complexities (Psychologically speaking in case that went a tad too far)

From an educated point of view, the Maslow's Hierarchy of Needs is a pyramid that was designed by a famous psychologist, Abraham Maslow. It indicated that human beings are in the need for good self-esteem. The only real chase in life is the pursuit of happiness (yeah, quote me), yet people are always on the lookout for fleeting highs and things unnecessary to living. The thing that most people do not realize is that anything that lowers your self-esteem in the case can be ripped away from you instantaneously without the bat of an eyelid. Happiness and other valued qualities of a good life that make sense to everyone last the longest in relation to time.

Many parts of the world live this way, unfortunately, planning on how to get more rates or high investment portfolios, and this line of thought is encouraged by the capitalist movement in several parts of the world.

There are several other things that we detach ourselves from to make room for things that have no real meaning to us. The latter describes how much wealth one owns, how many friends one has, or how many people hold us dear to their hearts. Now, these are the things that leave us empty and void once they are all stripped away from us in a fleeting second. They are all smoke and mirrors and have no place in defining who we are as a person.

When one feels they have high self-esteem because of these material possessions, they are blatantly lying to themselves. Only the ego is being fed, and not the Freudian kinds of ego, mind you. This is the ego that blinds a soldier going into war only to kill them in the waking process. These possessions make you feel so good about yourself, and they never want you to let them go. The devil's deal you see. The more you hold on to them, the more 'fulfilled' you feel.

This is where and how jealousy comes into play in this. Coupling yourself with these fleeting highs births jealousy as a byproduct. In the defining moment where you find yourself close to losing these material possessions, heavy negative emotion washes over you. The fear of loss is a powerful one, and this might be why people have a strong reaction while trying to catch the wind; the wind, in this case, is the material wealth.

How to deal with this materialism:

- You've already taken the first step. Acknowledging you have a problem is the first step. Second, you are already aware that self-worth is more important than placing value in materialistic ventures.

- Always ask yourself, if the materialistic ventures were not there, would you still feel good or even great about yourself? Plainly being alive and existing in this world is enough to make you worth something, and just as equal to anything valuable in the world.

- Your value is placed on the good things you can do in this world and how amazing your contribution, be it magnanimous or so small it cannot be seen, can be.

- Keeping this as a constant reminder can go a long way in improving your self-esteem, your self-worth, and seeing the worth in others as well. All the joy and laughter and music and wonder all depend on whether you decide to let all the materialism go and embrace your true inner self with no chance of reward or witness. In the words of Andy Dufresne, "They can never take what is in your mind. What's there is yours forever."

b.) Who you are as a person being put in the same category with random achievements.

There is a certain unspoken rule of thumb in never associating feelings of self-worth with fleeting highs such as money or the number of socks you have in your drawer. However, it should NEVER be considered to liken who you are as a person to ANYTHING remotely resembling anything.

There is no such thing as being a prick to get a service because of who you are, or from whom you were sired from or what you have done in your life. You still breathe the same air and drink water, just like the rest of people do.

Jealousy comes in the case where a young man who thought his relationship with his significant other would end in marriage, but it abruptly ended. This would lead to a case of lost identity, as he would now wonder what to do with himself. In the case where a person used to wearing the trending fashionable footwear and finds themselves in a position where they cannot afford to buy the expensive shoes anymore would find themselves in agony wondering what happened to their life.

This fixing of labels on our daily lives affects us in every way it can, even when we have no idea it is. It is almost as if one is in critical condition in the ICU and is closer to dying than breakfast roadkill. The level of ego one has to be in order to get this far is unfathomable, and a passionate retaliation to losing yourself to material lifestyles is commonly heard of and experienced.

How to deal with this level of egoistic tendencies:

Several quotes and books have been spoken and written to signify the bond of searching for your true soul. Climb that mountain. Take that road trip alone or with your dog. Adopt a dog. Learn a new style to cooking or fixing your roof. Ensure that the jealousy that could come up because of fear of losing yourself to material things comes to pass and never catches up with you ever again.

Here is the thing to hold dear in the hard times when you need a word of wisdom and your mind can't come up with cool Gandhi quotes; the person who you portray to the outside world is not you. The title you have at work is not the real you. The role you have in your organization is not you. The person you portray at home is not you. The person you act out to be is not you. The pain and suffering and joy and sorrow that happen to you are not you either. Only the spark, the consciousness that is inside of you is you.

c.) Low self-esteem

Solemn and glum souls reflect on the outside. Sometimes the people with this dark cloud hovering above them feel undeserving of the good things that life has to offer and may be more in fear of losing whatever good thing they have left than the next guy. In this situation, you might find the great guy with unfortunate self-esteem issues, who has the really cute girl may be inclined to be overly protective and jealous of even the coffee man.

The same can apply to friendships, with people becoming overprotective, jealous, and controlling in an attempt to keep their friends from abandoning them.

Neediness makes people with low self-esteem hold on more tightly to the things they have, and react with jealousy if they perceive a risk of it being taken away from them.

The things that make people have issues of low self-esteem are covered in chapter three of this book, but in the spirit of clarification and being thorough, one of the leading factors is a loose relationship with the caregivers who could be parents or guardians or older siblings, or seeing friends achieve something you wished to achieve but could not, like getting into a serious relationship that could potentially lead to marriage.

Constantly finding yourself to be a judgmental person can make it increasingly difficult to sustain relationships for a long time. It can even make it achingly painful to see someone who you thought of and called out as a failure succeeding in life, while there you are, stuck in the same place for years on end. Low self-esteem can result from this if not nipped in the bud early enough.

Reminding yourself each time you wake up along with the daily morning mantras that no one is ever above or below you, regardless of what they have accomplished in life, will help you see life in a deeper perspective and to always have something to look forward to.

It is important to you, dear reader, that you know that your lack of 'success' has nothing to do with your personality. Success is in quotes to put into context that the definition of the word is dependent upon the person using it. And to be quite honest, success is overrated anyway. The works of achievements that others have accomplished have nothing on you either. Just be strong as you are and fight the good fight.

Low self-esteem issues coupled with the narcissistic tendency to place achievements first and use them as a means to feel great about yourself may mean it's time to change your tire. Jealousy will creep up on you really soon.

d.) Belief that anger and spite will get you the results you want

Ever since anyone can remember their memories as a child, bad habits were rewarded with negative comments from our parents and/or guardians. It came sometimes with a bit of hiding (thanks mom and dad, for most of us wouldn't be here without you).

In lieu of this, we accepted our mistakes and took full responsibility for our actions (not entirely, but there was no other choice. Oliver Twist was just a fairy tale and the streets were harder). It only, therefore, made sense then that if you're angry (a common ingredient of jealousy), you always get what you want. Even if we don't acknowledge this belief consciously, there may be a part of us that believes that if we react to a situation with angry jealousy, somehow it will succeed in getting us what we want.

3. Jealousy and spiritualism. Are they linked?

a.) The mentality that there are differences in being among different people.

There is a theme in the America that we are all indoctrinated to believe, that we are all entities floating in the winds of the universe waiting for divine intervention to lead us along the path of righteousness. Children are encouraged when still young to be unique and to always be the first and win.

Due to this case of 'individualism', we tend to believe some of us are not worthy of the rights and privileges we enjoy. This deprives us of the joy of oneness, breeding hate and jealousy because of the thought that we deserve better than others. This is a tendency often seen in political rallies where one candidate beats the others down by saying how better he or she is.

Achieving oneness through thinking like a hive mind.

A hive mind can be related to how bees live and coexist with one another. They follow a certain sense of hierarchy and respect the rules of the system. They all have one collective agenda- to serve their queen. Spiritualism offers a conviction that we as humans are part of a hive mind. Rather than be as we are today, entangled in individualism and conceit, it explains that there is a thread connecting all of us into one unit. Think of it like the Musketeers from old France with their creed. Seeing the world through this eye glass can open you up to a world of endless possibilities. Your friend's success ultimately becomes your own success, and you will strive to help them achieve it, and in your own way be successful too.

This, in reality, takes jealousy out of the equation.

b.) Tricking the mind into hunger.

What this entails is tricking the mind into believing that there is a lack of resources out there and that only you were meant to go out and take it all for personal gain and use. Resentment can clearly come off of this, as well as jealousy, and this can be found quite frankly in over ambitious people.

Dealing with this appropriately:

Luckily, this is a mentality that can be tweaked and put into our control. It is a choice, you see, a choice to see the world as an abundance of infinite resources with enough to go around for everyone. When your neighbor is passed on to get a good fortune, then your chance of being in luck as he or she is still the same, and it is only for you to go out there and find it.

Spiritually speaking, if you really look for something and truly want it badly, the universe shall give it unto you. It is the universal law of Ask and It shall be given unto you. It does not only work in the old biblical days.

Try it and see some great things happen in your life.

c.) Law of attraction gone wrong.

In some cases, some people find themselves attracting the wrong mentalities and focusing on the wrong ideologies that may make them get jealous in turn. This is because they focus on getting their fears more than what would bring them happiness.

Positivity is the only way to counter bad vibes. Think and breathe like a child and you shall never be disappointed.

CHAPTER 5

TRIGGERS OF JEALOUSY

A breach of trust and several other qualities as will be discussed below leads to the creeping in of jealousy. Trust goes both ways; to others and to oneself. Let's look into some of the triggers of jealousy in detail;

The fear of being replaced

Being threatened by certain situations breeds jealousy. A form of jealousy is sibling jealousy that is caused by the irrational fear that their parents will love any one of their other siblings more than them. Most commonly seen in romantic affairs, jealousy is triggered by a third person, who does not necessarily impose a threat, but their mere presence is enough to bring in the green-eyed monster.

Those who live in fear are afraid to lose what they hold most dear to themselves as they, unfortunately, do not think they have what it takes to get it back or something better. This, in turn, makes them clingy and possessive, and quite possibly, dangerous.

Individual mentality

Individuality is as spontaneous as cow glue. Prior experiences of relationships gone wrong increase the likelihood of particular individual cases getting jealous. When a person has gone through a tough heartbreak more than once in a relationship prior to the current one, it will be quite difficult for them to go all out and love or trust someone like that ever again. It might be that they might commit to a relationship, but they will never let their guard down and accept to be hurt like that in the future. Case example being a person who was cheated on before; they will not let go of suspicion easily. Traits such as apprehension can also affect jealousy. People who tend to worry a lot are more likely to worry about losing a loved one.

The quality of the relationship

The occurrence of an explosive case of jealousy may arise when one is in doubt of the love a loved one gives them. It is a choice to love someone in a way that makes the relationship never lose its gusto; it is even better if the parties involved in the relationship wholeheartedly agreed to try their best to make it work. In the case of an unstable relationship, such as where the long distance calls become more and colder, the volatility may start to take shape. Volatile relationships tend to bring about this in many individuals making them highly prone to jealousy. Indeed, since jealousy is the fear of losing someone to another person, it may become unhealthy in the long term. For those relationships which are already a sinking ship, it is more important to note that jealousy may be the last hole to take it to the heart of Davy Jones' Locker. How two or more people relate in a relationship speaks volumes of how and when the jealousy may find its way into their connection.

CHAPTER 6

THE 7 LADDERS TO SMOOTHLY OVERCOME JEALOUSY IN A RELATIONSHIP

Smoothly overcoming jealousy may seem like an impossible task due to hurt feelings and painful backlash of words between partners, but it can be achieved through patience, perseverance and sticking to the following few steps:

1) This might sound a little cliché, but how about you believe your partner once in a while?

Surely this must be wrong, you might think, but why not take their word for it? Remember that if they do lie to you in your face, then they are only making a fool out of themselves. Trust is the foundation of every relationship, and it would be quite insulting of you to your significant other if you always give a shred of doubt with them at all times. Frequent buggering can be quite destructive as cheating in the long term.

Of course, you will still not trust your significant other for a while out of common routine, but the vigor to act as if you do believe them will rise from within. When they say they love you, believe them, and stop checking in at all times if they're where they say they are or with whom. Try your best to pretend to believe them, and with time they will see the sense of being honest with you. Eventually, the lies will stop, and a seamless sailing will occur.

2) Hark the wisdom knocks and says unto thee; quit comparing yourself to others.

Not all jealousy is driven by low self-esteem, but some are. None of us is ever going to comprehend why another person loves us. It's like arguing out if Siri, Apple's Artificial Intelligence for iPhones, knows what diverse implications it could cause if someone was to ask why their milk is frothy when boiled. Consider this my friend; that there are much better people than just about any one of us out there, but your significant other chose you because of that underlying spark inside you that they could not find anywhere else or with anyone else. The most notable people in history are way low on the list of looks or wealth, so stop worrying about working out why they could ever want to be with you.

3) It is wise to always prepare for everything, including preparing yourself to lose them.

It is not the best idea or thought to have, but it is a wise one. Not all jealousy is experienced by people with low esteem, for even those with high self-esteem are ranked to have the most intense levels of jealousy. This is so because they always have a tendency of being the center of the universe. Such flavors of people tend to have a view of people as material possessions, and quite right have the contentment to "share " their "property", not for a smile or a look at any other person at all. It is highly likely that they were spoiled brats as children.

It is a point to cautiously note that people are not playthings or toys to be constantly protected. To love someone or something you must be willing and ready to let them go at whatever the cost. Once you have accepted the fact that your actions might be the cause for the abrupt end of your relationship, it would be a good strategy to air it out with your partner. If all else fails, amicably agree to let bygones be bygones and part your ways in a friendly way.

Really, is this so? You ask, but wait, there's more to justify these claims;

Overprotective nature, anger, and jealousy drive love away fast, and love needs courage and bravery as spices to prosper. There is the natural fear of losing someone you hold dear to you, and obviously how that will make you feel. When imagination comes to play in this case, stretch that glorious mind into working out a scenario where the worst has happened and you are still alright. Not just alright, but flourishing in that imagined scenario.

Visualize about how well you would react in that situation, and keep playing back that Kelly Clarkson jam in your mind,"What doesn't kill you makes you stronger"

A hush point to note...keep this list in your memory palace, and not anywhere your significant other can find it. We don't want them feeling insecure, now do we?

4) Never consider even fathoming to play games. It's that serious.

We all know how uncomfortable jealousy makes the average person. It is unfortunate that people try to make themselves feel better by making their significant others jealous of them. Whoever coined the term 'Two can play that game' was holistically wrong on the matter. Never do this. All it does is lower the respect your partner has for you and degrades the love they have for you in the long term.

It is quite alright to have a look at that eye candy going down the block, but never use it as firepower to attack your partner. They say that if someone calls you names it should never hurt you; even if it does, you can take the comfort of knowing that their words reflect themselves and are not in any way a reflection of you.

5) Quit replacing reality with building castles in the sky.

Imagination is a powerful tool that creates scenes of your significant other cheating on you and propounds jealousy in huge doses. We as humans are so much bigger on the inside and can never get bored at all if we allow the exploration of the imagination station. If I sit back and imagine myself having a drink with Johnny Depp and spaceship lands on the patio and an alien with a burrito for a hand stumbles out, I have the pleasure of imagining it and doing whatever I want with that line of that, but it doesn't mean that I believe it.

Say for example, your partner is home later than you thought they were going to be, the moment you take the steps not to become emotional with imagined scenarios of your significant other cheating on you, that is the moment you have taken a bold step into overcoming jealousy.

6) Give them a little more rope.

Not to hang themselves (Jeez no!), or make a lasso with it (though this would be cool on another scale), but some space. Give your partner space. If your significant other wants to visit their friends from way back in college or long lost friends from back home, let them. They are their own individuals and have the right to do as they please. If you do not let them lead their own lives they will feel like hostages and will want to escape from that life you are giving them. Let them be free as they should, but this is not an excuse to let them walk over you. If you find yourself suspecting your significant other of trying to make you jealous, curb this by being chill about it, and be the better person and nip it in the bud. Talk to them, and before that, make it as spicy as you can. The situation could be used to your advantage and rekindle the flame of passion.

How? You may ask...by following step number 7.

7) Making beautiful use of that imagination to make you feel better, and not uncomfortably worse.

7 STEPS TO DEAL WITH JEALOUSY

Since seven is the lucky go-to number when gambling or finding the best playlist on a road trip or praying for a great week, here is a list of 7 phases or stages, if you will, to deal with jealousy. It is wise to note your bravery for being at this stage of discovery. From the following scenarios, you understand you have the feeling of jealousy with your partner, and now want to be better than your emotions.

1. Take a wise step back and evaluate your relationship.

Arguably one of the best ways to overcome jealousy is to first and foremost take a step back and assess your relationship. What this implies is to purposefully reflect on the foundation of your relationship, and consider if your partner's behavior reflects upon these values, be it trust, intimacy, commitment, or communication. A breather is always considered the healthiest way to come to terms with reality and grasp the implications of actions to be taken in the future.

If you feel they are not truly being honest with you, this can trigger a bout of insecurities. This is where it might get ugly. A lack of communication with your partner will always lead to this. Most fathers and sons rarely bond because of this, accrediting it to being manly and not talking about what they feel until it's too late for the relationship. A wise decision would be to come to terms with the fact that time moves regardless of good tidings or terrible moments, and it would be best to make the most of it.

When you find yourself in an insecure relationship, you should always expect your buttons to be pushed when it comes to jealousy. There is no one who can advise you on what to do but you. Staying will definitely leave you feeling terrible and very jealous almost all the time.

2. Take a breather and self-assess.

When you find yourself feeling insecure and untrusting in a relationship that has a solid foundation and is built on trust and honesty, you really need to take a glass of cold water, find a nice tree, like one that jumped right out of a Robert Frost poem, and sit under it with a good book and a picnic blanket to reevaluate your purpose in that relationship. It might be necessary to take a day off for this.

Perhaps you might find yourself to be a little too attached than usual, and this could be the reason to have such inclinations of jealous responses. Don't you worry; you are not alone in this.

There are those who have developed safe and secure attachments with their loved ones along their early years, and these are the ones who are inclined to be less jealous and clingy, have glowing social tendencies and high self-esteem, coupled with fewer feelings of inadequacy.

It is imperative to ask yourself these questions when it comes to that point of self-discovery:

- Does your soul feel empty and filled with a void?

- How were previous relationships with loved ones?

- How was the environment back at home? Warm? Loving? Heated?

- Was your upbringing a harsh one filled with repression?

- When you were a child were your guardians undependable?

The levels of attachment vary from person to person, and much later in life experiences and circumstances influence that level.

3. Always ask for help.

You're not being weak by doing so. You have friends, church help group, your local garbage man, or you can even find a random stranger. Talk to them. Problems half shared are problems half solved. Talk to someone other than your partner if you need a second opinion, but always consider talking about your feelings to your partner.

4. Accept that you are jealous.

Acceptance is the door to a happier life. Admitting that you are jealous opens a door to learning, and healing. Think of it like church, or anyone who has any seed of faith- naming the evil makes it lose its potency since one is no longer letting it humiliate them.

5. Lick your wounds and learn from that misstep.

Jealousy is an opportunity to go higher and move stronger. The moment you realize your friend writes excellent programs and creates amazing websites, instead of wallowing in jealousy and self-pity, you sign up for coding and graphic design classes.

6. Let the pain go and manage your feelings in a healthy manner.

In the words of the Doctor (no relation, only wishful thinking...), take all that pain and negativity and jealousy in your hand and put a fist around it, and say - never again. Breathe in and tell yourself you don't need that kind of bad vibe flowing through you. Let it go like a fart in the wind, never to be seen again. The best part is you can repeat it as many times as you want. Fun, isn't it?

Calmness is letting words and insults and emotions wash over you like water over stone. Taking in several breaths at a time help one detach from intense emotions. It is necessary to share feelings of deep jealousy after you calm down.

Sometimes all one needs is to get their gears rolling. Take a jog or a walk or write it down in a journal.

7. Always keep a reminder of your good side.

We all have a yin and yang, a good side and bad side and strength and weaknesses. Again, jealousy is a normal reaction. It becomes difficult to deal with when it becomes constant.

A point to note is to try your best to avoid alcohol or illegal drugs, as well as caffeine when experiencing stressful emotions. They tend to exaggerate mood swings and increase the chances of acting inappropriately.

CONCLUSION

In summary, as all good things come to an end, it is quite classical to review what the matter at hand is, and its drastic effects on life as an unchecked emotion. From the early days of mythology to the current century, jealousy still haunts our very being and meaning as a human race. The autonomy of belief in the thread that connects us all is quite strong in religious and spiritual grounds.

Jealousy is a disease, as well as a cure. This can be quite ironic, coming from the source of all good things reputable. Clearly, the human race needs to work on the relationship standards, before we can say we are fully developing into a universal oneness.

We have delved deep into the emotion that spells fear, doubt, clouds judgment, and destroys relationships. We have also seen how the wise can use this emotion to get ahead in building their relationships, breed trust, and enhance friendships and familial bonds with their siblings and parents.

Therefore the next time you get the chance with your significant other to play the jealous victim role, always put yourself in their shoes and mull over some few thoughts;

Are these feelings new?

Could it not be the first time they're acting this way?

It is imperative to note that someone with a tendency and nature to be obsessive and controlling even in their previous relationships will not go down easy. Time and a lot of it will be spent in much-needed therapy sessions with a professional. You will be lucky to find a partner willing to change and take the steps necessary to take control of their emotions.

It would be wise to say that using everything at hand, including emotions as a tool to make things better in our daily lives, is a skill learned and should be used at every opportunity when necessary.

Chances to be overwhelmed with jealousy should be overcome by taking heed to the steps outlined in this book, as well as taking the chance to repair the cracks in any relationship. The beginning and end of a relationship is a choice. One chooses to love another, and should, therefore, be prepared to take on any hurdle to come their way, including painful moments of emotion, and learn to use that obstacle to build something better than it was before.

Thank you!

Before you go, I just wanted to say thank you for purchasing my book.

You could have picked from dozens of other books on the same topic but you took a chance and chose this one.

So, a HUGE thanks to you for getting this book and for reading all the way to the end.

Now I wanted to ask you for a small favor. **Could you please take just a few minutes to leave a review for this book?**

This feedback will help me continue to write the type of books that will help you get the results you want. So if you enjoyed it, please let me know! (-:

Also, don't forget to grab a copy of your Free Bonus book "*How to Talk to Anyone: 50 Best Tips and Tricks to Build Instant Rapport*". If you want to increase your influence and become more effective in your conversations then this book is for you.

CPSIA information can be obtained
at www.ICGtesting.com
Printed in the USA
BVHW040738201119
564176BV00032B/347/P

9 781951 754297